Instructions for Folding

SERIES EDITORS

Chris Abani

John Alba Cutler

Reginald Gibbons

Susannah Young-ah Gottlieb

Ed Roberson

Instructions for Folding

Poems

Willie Lin

NORTHWESTERN UNIVERSITY PRESS

EVANSTON, ILLINOIS

Northwestern University Press
www.nupress.northwestern.edu

Northwestern University Poetry and Poetics Colloquium
www.poetry.northwestern.edu

Printed in the United States of America

10   9   8   7   6   5   4   3   2   1

Library of Congress Cataloging-in-Publication Data

Lin, Willie, author.
  Instructions for folding : poems / Willie Lin.
    pages cm. — (The Drinking gourd chapbook poetry prize)
  ISBN 978-0-8101-3103-3 (pbk. : alk. paper)
  I. Title. II. Series: Drinking gourd chapbook poetry prize.
PS3612.I518I57 2015
811.6—dc23

2014038243

Contents

Foreword

CHRIS ABANI

The idea of folding, of creases and blemish, is fundamental in the world of books. The medium is paper and paper has long been cherished for its flaws, its imperfections, all of which give it a singular identity—a beauty which we find in the object of the book itself. The cracking of a cover, the scent of ink and resin, the curious opaque loop of print that is in fact a window onto a vastness create a fetish which is half the joy of reading. There is also the delight of folding the page to mark your place, to hold an inner fold in yourself.

In this book we encounter an origami of identity, love, place, relationship, and trauma mediated in a language that attempts transformation, that succeeds at renegotiation. We quite simply fold along the spine, crease, and begin unfolding, and with each reading a lingering pattern of lines and creases is left that, in complicated ways, maps the path away from and back to the object that we begin with. Wrapped tightly at the heart of this book is a question that is almost too much to ask—if it is to mean anything, if we are to know the unknowable, even about our own experiences, how do we begin?

The folding that happens in this collection of poems is a complex art of obscuration and revelation, hidden sometimes in beguilingly simple turns. Difficulty, trauma, and the transformation of these into something extraordinary are often the subject of poems. Lin's book makes an important distinction: it's the way in which language here plays subtly against chords of pain, revealing, in the most mesmerizingly simple forms, a dark turn and an unspeakable thing.

There are moments of stunning honesty that resonate. Here, for example, are the opening interrogative lines of "An Aria": "I don't want to be an aggrieved person, then I think, / What other kind is there?" Or in "Celebration," Lin reveals a disarming and endearing vulnerability: "I had very good, if not the best of, intentions. Everyone in the audience / was in love."

The book is unflinching in accounting for the daily cruelties of our lives, the melancholy of it. In "Elegy for Misremembered Things," Lin rightly wrestles with the unreliability of some of our most important sources for sentiment and poetry—memory and its less reliable double, nostalgia: "What is ordinary sorrow? / The days settle like snow"—and the inability of memory and nostalgia to rework anything satisfactorily. And yet because of this, all the moments of wonder and delight in these poems—and there are many—are hard won and believable.

This is an important debut for a poet who will only get stronger and stronger with every book, with every new poem. And so we succumb to the grace of the fold, the redemption of paper, the mapping and charting of ink and joy.

Acknowledgments

Grateful acknowledgment goes to the editors of the following publications, in which some of these poems first appeared, sometimes in slightly different forms:

Broadsided: "To You and For You"
Handsome: "Passage"
RHINO: "Dream with Omen"
Washington Square Review: "Teleology"

Thanks, also, to *Paperbag* for the prompt that led to the title poem.

Thank you Lisa Russ Spaar. Thank you Jennifer Chang, Marni Ludwig, Philip Matthews, Carl Phillips, Allan Popa, Shi-Shi Wang, and Sara Yenke.

Love and heartfelt thanks to Joe Collins and my family.

Instructions for folding:

The dictum is that we must experience personally the impersonal.
Mountain ash, white calyx of snow, tall wind whipping, the perfected

order of the circadian world. Raise a hand and eclipse
a whole field, the dull blade deadeye of memory.

I asked myself, Are my interests intellectual or sentimental?
Is time an event or a condition? I was and am ill, if I'm to be believed.

To You and For You

In the dream I was abducted, I thought sleep
would save me. That's how dumb I was, how mulish.
I thought my sleep would stop them. When the man
whispered in my ear, *If you so much as make one sound*—
the words were so soft I tried to pretend I hadn't heard
him, and his warm hand across my face hadn't disturbed me
from sleep. I thought of bees locked in amber, the curlicues
of their antennae inert but preserved in attention. I thought
hives must be fear in miniature, a swarming of infinitesimal
hooks and combs with its own scent and rhythm. Who was I
I knew I was useless, incapable in that moment of acting even
to save myself, nor even wanting to. I wanted to sleep
until the danger passed, as if it were separate from me.

Passage

i. When visitors come we oversalt the stew

Good as dead
was not an expression we understood.

Because there were visitors, we added more salt to our stew &
    offered no water
so thirst would circumscribe appetite,

though we were soon sorry
for our poverty. The visitors brought:

> All the delineated beauties of a horse—
> the fine nose & mane, the fine eyes, almost human.

> Perfect pitch & leather lungs, with which they sang for us
> songs so cheerful we thought we were mistaken to be sad.

> A lullaby for their children—

we were shy around other children, especially
ones not yet capable of speech, so empty of guile.

The visitors said we held a charm like water music & explained the sea—
    we learned
to want its presence, its profound cool & hush, tides like
a woman's swell of breast & ache of spine.

So little happened here—
some days passed with a sky the color of smoke, some days the
    color of sand—

it seemed remarkable we had stayed so long, we seemed to the visitors &
    then to ourselves
    persons of remarkable patience & passivity.

& though we were not superstitious—
did not believe in gods or ghosts, not by such terms—we thought

we were constantly at the edge of ourselves, in danger
of asking too much, & in so doing risked losing everything.

ii. Bellwether

Never a question of belonging to
or of freedom from—

at last it was more difficult than we thought to be without ambition.
We had thought it our penitential duty as the forsaken

to stand very still, at times, to keep the world close, but animals
had moved away from us anyway, moved, like us, by hunger & whim—

need & pleasure
or something resembling it—& their feathers kept catching on our
    hearts' blades.

Our bodies, being mostly water, shared some of its qualities:
so much dissolved in us

without changing us: unmoored, we moved with an ease that looked like
determination—

iii. On the other side

We woke too early or much too late
& thought the world had become golden.

Both wind & its absence
seemed signs—the way it lifted

our hair & goaded us
helpfully onward, the way

stillness hinted we ought to listen
closer. We assured each other

we were not alone, & felt reassured.

Then we said to ourselves the opposite,
which seemed no less true.

When night came it was distant & intimate:
its fall full of gaps & breaths

yet dense. It was difficult to tell
if its obscurity

meant we were lost in thought's bramble
or bare-limbed at the heart of the matter.

I tried to brush an insect from
your skin, left
instead a clumsy streak of hull & viscera.

To prove I loved the world still, I told myself some lives were
too delicate to save, or too slight.

iv. Where there is smoke there is spire

Although it still seemed early
to declare loss,
it was late for victory.

There is time now to say what you've wanted
to hear.

Still Life with Nothing in It

Someone wants to die.
The day is gone.
Its brightness gone.

Its rocks among vacancy.
Damp greenery, coiled
heads of lilacs. Though

their small scent remains,
and the difficulty
remains. The dying will

invent again their truths
and treachery with
which they will not live.

Heat rises in hushed
sounds like paper ripping,
and your hands, taking up

the task, numinous as
crows folding themselves
into auspices of trees

and then awaying
in bursts, fit for
a cry, a clap of black

wings in pools of sky.
Self-hate, self-love,
always the inimical

self in the lostness.
Brittle tooth. Beautiful
things are becoming lost

all the time. Other things, too.

Epithalamium

Spring snow,
vast consolation of landscape. The man you love
turns to open the next gate.
All around, those who shape air
into the intended and unintended, a faint sweetness in
the bobbin unspooling its cord of blood.

Little Face

—for Marni, after Paul Sietsema's *At the Hour of Tea*

The background is a gradation of gray, straw, dust, and the shade of dull neglect found on the underside of leaves. A horse and a man are the dusk preceding black, flecked with the wrinkled pattern of the stone canvas. A horse carries a man. The bit, delicate but true. Each of the horse's legs swells as a separate, thick stroke though together they form a loose, convex array, almost arboreal. The horse's tail, a soft swipe, reveals motion through its high arc. The rider's feet dangle, one-two, below the animal's torso. He raises one arm, attendant toward the rein. The other arm curves behind him toward the animal's back. The man and horse move not through landscape but desolation, as if the hand that had painted them had lifted them from one life and dropped them into another in a hurry, undoing their meaning. They move in silhouette, in a silence preceding silence. The horse's perked ears are the smallest details. The horse's face, forehead to chin, pitch forward from the torso oblique on an achromatic path. Its direction is uncertain as a course, dissolving into what may be water or shadows. For all these, there is no rest for millennia. The days are shorter. *The distance is dark but full of color.*

Monday: fog

Tuesday: rain
Wednesday: night pouring a tall blue one

> I am writing from between two lakes
> of the weather report. Poor visibility for all.
> We none of us can see

(predict) tomorrow. Snowdrift snaking
across the ice. We think we can see below it, fish
swift and shadowless

> because their skin is light—
> illumination and counter-illumination.
> Very fancy. Very smart.

I am proud to report, we are all
appropriately in awe
of the cold as a faithful companion, indeed

> it occupies my mind
> day and night, day and night, you see.
> Should it be so hard

to carry on being ourselves?
Can you tell by looking at someone's gloved hand
whether and how it means to harm?

> When someone speaks
> or I speak into the air. What comes after
> the physical world? We are seeking—

> > not a boat, not dawn—
> > tired as we are (very tired) in gestures of repose

Elegy for Misremembered Things

What is ordinary sorrow?

The days settle like snow, visiting each thing, lending a sameness to
their shapes.

White on white.

Heavy is the head incapable of treachery.

A missing left index finger, the man whose hand it was.

He was stern. His hair never lost its shape. How many dead had he seen?

And you ask of the cat, "For once, will you cease thinking of yourself."

A yellow tinge in the sky. Sand from the desert blows south until the
air is full of sand. It tangles your hair. It fills your mouth. You cannot
sweep it from the concrete floor of the house.

Pour water down the steps and watch it cascade.

Watching it dry. Time was elastic.

A woman strikes your hand with a chopstick as it moves across a cold
music, ticking each mistake.

You were always alone. You were never alone.

The boy who pinned you to the bed and could not explain why. Your
matching uniforms, his red cheeks.

The singular, fluid motion of a man in a dark blue coat as he alighted his
bicycle. His confidence in that moment makes you cry.

The naked women at the public shower never stop talking.

Or you slipped through a gate to see the men and women in shapeless white striped shirts and pants outside the government hospital.

You could run the perimeter of your entire world without needing to stop.

A stranger thinks you look like a doll. A cartoon of a girl. She has never seen another like you. She wants to dress you in her military cap and take a photograph.

Later, it arrives in the mail.

Teleology

I am finely attuned to failures.
I am an instrument of them. I accept my failings
vis-à-vis the design and accept confusion
as my occupation because I am a student, not a scholar.
This is the only world. And I am to it undifferentiated
as a lump of stone (for whom identity is not a riddle,
and I recognize the superiority of the stone in this aspect).
I am allotted an amount of daylight and that amount
shifts daily not according to my failures qua failure
but another logic. I am allotted darkness also, the effect
of which I can reproduce in part by shutting my eyes.

Dream with Omen

A fish head is a good thing,
to be sure—prized

for its luster one might
swallow, its dead eyes like curdled milk—

one might carry it
with consideration, one might

kiss it for luck, hold it next to the ear
for a tinny music, ask of it

in the new year, *Where is my mother?*
Am I dead meat? Give it a little salt,

blood and hair. Allow me
to demonstrate how to chew the skin

from its lip, without
a look, without a cry—how to

hang the curtains, wear a dress
white as wonder, and twirl

the fishy smell like a ring around the finger.
By the water, I lost my mother.

By the water, someone left
a fish by the pillow as I slept

with a low lamp to feel watched over.
I asked the head, *Where is the center?*

The fish meant I was exhausted.
The head was a joke, a poor substitute.

I would like to rest now
with my head in a warm lap.

Byzantine

I walked to the city. The cold held my breaths briefly
before letting them die so I could see in their form the consequence
of something true. The darkened corolla

of heads bereft as islands. You can visit
their contents, see them all at once. To use such words
as from another's childhood: *demitasse, flussfisch* . . . I was busy hiding my
    errors.
I was also tired of the challenge.

In the small painting, the figures floating in gold
evince no distance—each pleasing to the eye, calm as colors
green, violet, blue, pale yellow, pink—

An Invention

A myth is at the same time imperfectible and unquestionable;
time or knowledge will not make it better or worse.

—ROLAND BARTHES

It's all downhill from here.   —MY FATHER

A father is unlikely to be a myth and yet

*

A man is dying in California.
My father.
Our father, I say on the phone to my sister.
Who art in California, I say, because he is now as distant and unknowable
    as a god.
As for his silence, I have come to prefer it.

*

I don't know about my father.
Habits: lifestyle. As in, which side of the bed
Habits: attire. As in, what he wears when

What do you mean? He used to love to ask.
What do you mean *the future isn't what it once was*?
What do you mean *that isn't the right question*?

*

I read a book for signs. So slow, light
across the house, my garden, and the woods beyond.

The book says,   is *a glance* from God.
First, I think, *attention*.
Then, *injury*.
For a long time.

Funeral

—But if you could keep anything of yourself.
—I wouldn't.

Walking, my sister in front of me, her hair blowing
into my face, madder
than thought. Later,
we will play a fugue blindfolded.
Hairpin turns
across hands.

Stereoscopy

Things explain each other, not themselves. —GEORGE OPPEN

Doubtful. —MY FATHER

When we were together, there were two works of art that W. loved above
 all others:
Brancusi's *Little French Girl II*
which was also called *Plato*
which later became *Tête*

                  & (contradiction)

                              Rauschenberg's *Erased de Kooning Drawing*
                                    a pretend homage but an actual
                                        palimpsest of nothing.

& what brings me back is the woman standing next to me in the portrait
gallery talking about her collection of animal skulls. *A fetish is a story
masquerading as an object*, an aphorism that proved truer each time W.
repeated it. Brancusi made *Little French Girl II* with an oak head, a long
rail-thin neck, unlovely feet, and a singular sense of what it meant to
be fleshly yet obsessed with the soul. Then he severed the head, made
it answer to *Head*, and renounced and threw out the rest of the body.
Rauschenberg made *Erased de Kooning Drawing* in one sly month, in a
process that was all rasp and snare and backtrack. He was trying to erase
himself into a history. A process a lot like snow falling on water.

Why? The woman's companion does not ask her of the nearly one hun-
dred skulls that she keeps on the bookshelves lining her office. *Yes, some
were gifts from family and friends.* I imagine her presiding over them. *Oh,
birds, cow, dogs—all sorts and sizes.* Learning their heft.

Stories about Us

What's your relationship to reality?
In my dreams, I am always human. Worse than that, I am always myself.
Astray. No, ashtray.

*

I have one great loneliness and many other
lonelinesses. My father believes I have a great mind because I asked
abstruse questions when I was five.

*

When you are young, there is nothing interesting
about you, though people are interested in you.
It is easy then to believe the opposite.

*

After you die, you do not cease being someone's child.
In history and actuality, you will always be so-and-so's son or so-and-so's
    daughter,
even after all the names in your particular story are forgotten.

*

I believe that it is not as they say.
Pain does not build character. Pain makes pain your familiar.
For example, this might be one difference between my father and me.

*

Do not let facts stop your feelings.

For example, I believe certain differences are differences. If you were W., you might believe all differences are important differences.

An Aria

I don't want to be an aggrieved person, then I think,

What other kind is there?

When I loved W., I thought he contained nearly all of the beauty the
world had to offer.

Hide and seek. Hymn and palinode.

To utter something is to gain a measure of control over what is being
revealed. A fact

W. was never shy about.

You will not be spared from the thing you love most. I index this under:
Quel dommage! Also, *It can't be helped!*

You know, W. said, I'm tired of this feigned self-pity, not everything can
be magnified

to tragedy through feeling. (I'm paraphrasing.)

This could have been the beginning or the end of one type of argument
we had.

Lean as a knife, narrow as the blade of one

is how Virginia Woolf described her father, or how she described Mr.
Ramsay.

She had a heart the shape of an ax

is how Lorrie Moore described one of her heroines.

I admire women who glance

and sharpen against the necessary difficulties, blade-to-whetstone. My
sister

thinks I am an unfaithful reader, liable

to mistakes of emphasis, traveling line by line by page by hour, wanting
only my own suspicions confirmed,

but I say I am guileless. The train that knows its course though the tracks
are obscured by snow.

Sehnsucht at the portrait gallery, *sehnsucht* at the laundromat with mis-
matched socks.

I'm embarrassing.

Living with W. was like living in a world in which the laws of causality
   are opaque:
Glance at the clock, and a hat falls from its hook.
Rearrange the chairs, and water courses down my throat.
Dog-ear the page, and someone departs.

Sunday Dinner

Because we like to arrive at a place of understanding,
we return. This is a beautiful photograph, I lie to my sister,
because of the perspective. The way the figures are central to a fault.

Now and not now.

Catachresis: language for the saddest things.

Isolato: in another life, we'd like to be celebrated for our bad timing.

Clean: nothing scours my floors like a bad memory,
one in which I am blameless and happy.

In the kitchen today, oil and soft cloth,
I wipe until I am what I feel: an honest exhaustion. By now
we are so far away from usefulness, my sister jokes.
Then she leaves me to my work.

Celebration

I had very good, if not the best of, intentions. Everyone in the audience was in love.

In the small town W. and I visited, a celebration: The Festival of Silence.

At night, a *ballet blanc* performed with no music, *en pointe*, a white toss of skirts like a consternation of clouds.

A Fugue

We're undone by each other. And if we're not,
we're missing something.   —JUDITH BUTLER

I don't remember.   —MY FATHER

He was an avid photographer.
My sister and I were frequent subjects
in childhood—

our curious twin heads,
our matching haircuts and dresses
at the piano bench, by the fountain, in the yard

bent to the good work of muddying our hands and knees.
And when he wasn't behind
the camera, he gazed past us

with a vague indifference. Conversation
bewildered him, though
he was full of aphoristic wisdom that he dispensed

regardless: When the going gets tough—
and so on.
Not an uncheerful man, he had seemed to me.

We were women who didn't know a thing
about discretion, was his assessment.
Not untrue, though by then his mind was already leaving him.

He recognized us for the strangers we always were.
The heart is muscle,
not memory,

but try telling me that even now, standing in my father's
old house. Every point
in the photograph hanging on the wall equally far

from the truth of our condition
then, living there.
Thumb to index finger, thumb to index finger—

with his hands framed as a viewfinder
was how my father preferred to move through the world,
eyes narrowed with what looked like purpose.

Harbor

From the bridge, we consider endings. We are faithful
in our concerns
if not original in our reproach—that the night is long, that someone else
is better loved,
will love better—
in the rank heat of summer, with the new flush of green tufts of trees
crowding the heart:
Who do you blame?
Who do you want to blame?
From this distance, we cannot see our reflections. For example, my sister
thinks
this sadness is a ruse.
All this bleakness on a bright day in parks
a deliberate will.
We argue not because we do not know what else to do, but because
this is what we do.
As girls, reading fairy tales to each other, my sister and I thought
because we were very beautiful,
we had been spared a terrible fate. Nor have we abandoned our desire
for simple stories.

Letters

I don't believe you.   —MY FATHER

Tautology.   —MY FATHER

I start a letter that I do not finish.
Or should I say diary although I have addressed it to others.
The addressees kept changing, and so
the quality of truth kept changing.

> *When I met W., he was sitting in an armchair*
> *in an alleyway, looking like one of those French men who burn*
> *cars. Dangerous—no. Yes and no.*
>
>   (Good.)

> *Who has that kind of confidence*
> *in their own perceptions of the world.*
> *Mad people.*
>
>   (Poor.)

> *They have other ideas about happiness.*
> *Father, as you know, has other ideas about happiness.*
> *When I think of him now, I think how nice it is*
> *to be always traveling away from oneself.*
>
>   (Poor.)

> *I know I am romanticizing. It is hard to imagine*
> *what anyone wants is less order. Stop.*
>
>   (False.)

*

(some law)
(in the mind)

(a hold)
(a hole)

*

> *The train rattled me from sleep in the dark I wanted to wake you*
> *by touching your temple down sleep's long corridor you'd hear me*
> *coming narrowly it seemed you were away but not beyond language*

Willie Lin lives and works in Chicago. Her poems have appeared in *1110*, *Blackbird*, the *Cincinnati Review*, *Washington Square Review*, and other journals.